Leila's Game

by Spike Breakwell and Colin Millar
illustrated by Moni Perez

Chapter 1

It was after school and the girls' basketball team were playing a game against another local school. Everyone in the team really enjoyed playing. The girls loved passing, catching and dribbling the ball. They all ran around the court as fast as they could.

3

The girls ran with the ball and bounced it at the same time. Mai was great at this. Amira was really good at catching the ball. She was taller than the other players. She scored points by throwing the ball into the basket. Zara was a fast runner and really keen to play well. She ran all over the court, catching the ball and passing to her team mates. Yet they hardly ever won a game.

Leila sat in her wheelchair on the side lines watching her school friends. She was happy watching her friends play even though she couldn't join in. She wished she could play too but knew she couldn't. She sat watching and cheering the loudest to encourage and support them.

They needed all the help they could get. Miss Garcia, who coached the team, knew this as well. She walked over to Leila.

'We don't seem to be doing very well again,
do we, Leila?' said Miss Garcia.

'No,' agreed Leila. 'I can't understand it.'

'Neither can I. They're fast enough
and keen enough. Maybe I haven't got them
playing in the right position. Oh well, maybe
next time!' Miss Garcia said, sadly.

Leila looked at the scoreboard. 'Oh dear',
she thought. 'Fourteen points down'.
Then she looked at the timer. There were only
five more minutes until the end of the game.

'Come on!' she shouted, trying to encourage her
friends to make a last big effort to win the game.

Afterwards, she sat with her friends as they drank their orange juice. They had lost the game. Everyone seemed sad and tired. Leila tried to cheer them up but it was no use. Leila knew there had to be a reason why her friends hadn't won the game. If only she could think of a way to help them start winning.

Leila turned to her best friend, Zara.
'Hard luck Zara,' she said, 'I thought you all played really well.'

'Thanks Leila,' replied Zara. 'I am disappointed, but thanks for the great support. You cheered louder than anyone.'

Leila smiled at her friend. She always wanted Zara to do well. She got excited when she saw Zara running fast or making a good pass. But she felt lonely on the side lines and desperately wanted to join in with her friends. She talked to Zara about this on the way home.

'I know Leila,' Zara said. 'We all want you to be able to play, too.'

Chapter 2

On Saturday morning, Leila wheeled her chair to the café in town to meet her grandfather. Every weekend, they would meet and play games outside the café. Sometimes they would play draughts. Sometimes they would play dominoes. Sometimes they would play ludo.

Leila was still thinking hard about how to help her friends when she arrived at the café. She saw her grandfather sitting at their usual table. She went over and gave him a big, happy hug.

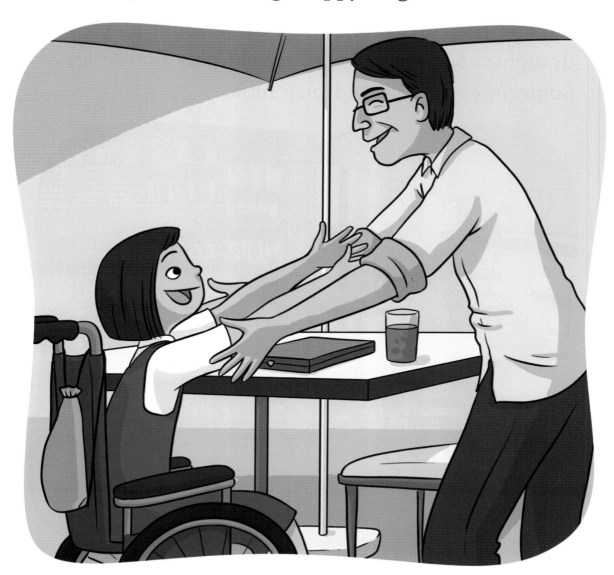

'Ah,' Grandfather smiled. 'Here's my wonderful granddaughter Leila!'

'Hello Grandfather,' Leila said. 'What game are we playing today?'

'Today, my little one, I shall teach you how to play backgammon,' he replied.

'What's backgammon, Grandfather?' Leila asked.

'It's a very old game that is based on strategy' said grandfather.

Leila wasn't sure what strategy meant, so she asked him.

'A strategy is a plan for how you're going to play a game,' said Grandfather. 'And having a strategy means you can change your plan if your opponent does something you don't expect. A good strategy helps you win the game. Do you understand?' Grandfather smiled down at Leila.

'I think so,' replied Leila, 'but I'm not sure how to start making my own strategy.'

'Ah-ha!' laughed Grandfather. 'That's the clever part. What you have to do is look at the different pieces on the board. Then decide on the best way to use them. You have to think about where to place the pieces to stop the other player winning. A good strategy involves thinking about all of the pieces on the board or all of the players in a team.'

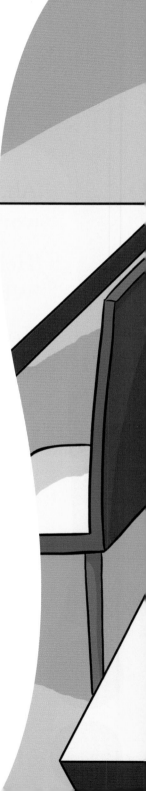

They began their game of backgammon. As they played, Leila kept thinking about Grandfather's brilliant idea of a strategy. This might be a way to help her friends.

'Grandfather?' Leila asked, thoughtfully. 'Would a strategy help my friends win a game of basketball?'

'Absolutely!' replied Grandfather. 'A good strategy, is based on what each member of the team does well. It helps them play better.'

'Thank you,' said Leila. She smiled as she moved her last piece on the board. 'And it looks like I've won the game!'

'Good gracious!' exclaimed Grandfather, laughing and clapping his hands. 'How ever did you manage that?'

'I had a strategy,' giggled Leila.

Chapter 3

By the time Leila got back to school after the weekend, she had a strategy to help her friends. Their next game was in two days' time. So, at break, she sat with them and told them about her strategy to play the game and win. It was all based on what her friends were good at.

'Zara is quick and can pass really well,'
Leila explained. 'So she passes to Mai. Then Mai
can use her dribbling skills to run down the side
of the court and pass back to Zara. And then Zara
passes to Amira who's the best at scoring baskets.
What do you think?'

Her friends stopped eating and looked at her.

'Brilliant!' said Mai.

'Awesome!' agreed Amira.

'What a great plan! Let's go and tell Miss Garcia straight away,' said Zara, getting up out of her seat.

Chapter 4

It was the day of the match. Miss Garcia smiled at Leila and then blew her whistle to begin the game. Leila cheered for her friends. Would her strategy work? Would Zara be able to get her pass to Mai? And would Mai be able to dribble past the other team's players?

Suddenly, Zara caught the ball.

'Zara pass to Mai,' Leila roared. She was getting excited. Now she would see if her plan would work.

Zara quickly passed the ball to Mai. Mai caught it and began bouncing it, running as fast as she could past the other players. Zara zoomed along the court ready to catch the ball back from Mai. Amira got herself into position, ready to try and score.

Leila held her breath. 'Nearly there', she thought. She wanted to keep on shouting and cheering but she didn't want to distract her friends.

Zara caught the ball again. She made a great pass to Amira, who leapt up into the air towards the hoop. Amira threw the ball. It curved high up into the air for what seemed to be the longest time, before dropping straight through the hoop.

'Hurrah!' everyone cheered. Leila threw both arms into the air and shouted louder than she had ever shouted before.

The rest of the game went by in a flash. Leila's strategy worked superbly and her friends won by nine points.

Afterwards, Miss Garcia congratulated the team.

'We wouldn't have won without Leila's great plan,' said Zara.

'You're quite right, Zara,' smiled Miss Garcia. 'In fact, Leila did so well I have decided that she should be the joint coach for the team. What does everyone think?'

The whole team cheered and clapped. Leila beamed a big, proud smile as Miss Garcia handed her a cap with **Coach** printed across the front.

The next game, Leila found herself in charge of the team. Miss Garcia let her make the decisions. She worked out a strategy beforehand. During the game she shouted instructions, changing the strategy to match what the other team was doing.

It was a close game but Leila's friends won and everyone cheered.

The team all gave Leila a *high five* as they came off the court. Miss Garcia shook Leila's hand. 'Well done again, Leila. You are a great coach and a great addition to the team.'

'Thanks Miss Garcia,' said Leila, 'I love coaching the team, but I still really would love to be able to play as well.'

'You can,' said Miss Garcia. 'A new wheelchair basketball club has started on the other side of town. I have told them all about you and your coaching skills. They were impressed with your strategies. They want you to join their mini-basketball team ... as a player!'

'Brilliant! We can all come and cheer Leila on for a change!' laughed Mai. 'What a great end to a great day!' Leila was so excited. She couldn't wait to go along to the new club and begin playing basketball.

Chapter 5

Three weeks later, Tefo, Pelo, Omar and the girls all stood on the side lines as the whistle blew. Like lightening, Leila spun her chair neatly around to catch the ball. This was her first game and she was very excited.

'Come on Leila!' her friends cheered.

Leila wheeled her chair as fast as she could, past the other players and passed to her team mate. She turned her chair again and zipped into position near the basket. The ball was passed back to her. She took careful aim. Her friends held their breath. Leila threw the ball perfectly straight. Whoosh! It dropped through the hoop without even touching the sides.

Everyone cheered and clapped as Leila turned, giving her friends a huge grin. She looked over at the crowd and saw her grandfather waving and cheering at his very clever granddaughter.

This truly was Leila's game.

Leila's Game ☞ Spike Breakwell and Colin Millar

Teaching notes written by Sue Bodman and Glen Franklin

Using this book

Content/theme/subject

In this story, Leila is worried about her friends in the basketball team. They keep losing their games. A discussion with her grandfather gives her an idea, and she is able to help them plan a strategy using the strengths of each team member. The story tackles familiar themes of friendship and problem-solving, with a satisfying resolution.

Language structure

- The text provides clear layout of direct speech with punctuation to aid reading aloud with expression and meaning.
- Sentences are longer with two or three clauses, providing information about characters and events to support comprehension.

Book structure/visual features

- Events occur over time and place, supported by chapter breaks and illustrations.

Vocabulary and comprehension

- New and specific vocabulary is introduced in a strong, supportive context.
- A variety of verbs are used in reporting clauses e.g. 'smiled', 'asked', 'replied' on p.13.

Curriculum links

History – Backgammon is thought to be one of the oldest board games, at about 5,000 years old. Children could explore the history of board games played in their country.

Maths – Explore the rules of probability with dice, for example what number combination will occur most in 20 rolls of the dice?

Learning outcomes

Children can:

- note how dialogue is presented in a range of styles.
- make sensible predictions, justifying these with evidence from the text and from prior knowledge.
- hold story events in their heads during a reading lesson, learning to recall significant facts/ideas when reading the same text over more than one lesson.

Planning for guided reading

Lesson One: Dialogue conventions to support comprehension

Ask the children to predict the type of story, based on what they know already of these characters. The story will also stand-alone, and is not dependent on having read others in the International School strand.

On p.4, explore the skills required in basketball.

On p.6, take the children to the line: *'No,' agreed Leila. 'I can't understand it.'* Ensure that children understand that Leila continues talking after the reported clause. Ask the children to find other places where the author has used this writing technique (e.g. on p.9). Draw attention to how these sentences are punctuated (use of speech marks and commas).

Give a quick overview of the remaining events of Chapter 1, picking up on the team's disappointment (p.8) and Leila's wish to be able to play (p.10).

On p.14, Grandfather explains the use of 'strategy'. This is pivotal to the story. Have the children read this page quietly to themselves, and ensure they can explain what a strategy is.